"... because each is
special and precious"

To Gay
and Uncle Ralph

From Susan

Love,
Christmas 1998

THE JOY OF
CHRISTMAS

A SEASON
OF WONDER

Publications International, Ltd.

Louis Weber, C.E.O.
Publications International, Ltd.
7373 North Cicero Avenue
Lincolnwood, Illinois 60646

Permission is never granted for commercial purposes.

Manufactured in China.

8 7 6 5 4 3 2 1

ISBN: 0-7853-2827-0

Gail Dodge is a seasoned writer who has written for dozens of publications and organizations. She is the author of *A Bristol Falls Christmas Carol* and *Nativity Stories,* among other titles. She is a frequent contributor to *Joy of Collecting* magazine.

Acknowledgments:
Publications International, Ltd., has made every effort to locate the owners of all copyrighted material to obtain permission to use the selections that appear in this book. Any errors or omissions are unintentional; corrections, if necessary, will be made in future editions.

Page 8: "I Am the Christmas Spirit" by E. C. Baird excerpted from *The Ideals Classic Christmas Treasury.* Used with permission from Thalia Baird in memory of E. C. Baird. Page 16: Excerpt from *At Christmas the Heart Goes Home* by Marjorie Holmes, 1991, used with permission from the author. Page 25: Reprinted from *The Scented Christmas* © 1991 by Gail Duff. Permission granted by Rodale Press, Inc., Emmaus, PA 18098. Page 26: "Circled with Light" reprinted from *WinterSong* by Madeleine L'Engle and Luci Shaw, © 1997. Used by permission of Harold Shaw Publishers, Wheaton, IL 60189. Pages 32–33: Excerpt from "Legend of the Flower" by Francis X. Weiser from *The Christmas Book,* 1952, used with permission from the Society of Jesus New England. Page 37: From *The Merriest Christmas Book* by Mark Link, S.J. © 1974, RCL Enterprises, Inc., Allen, TX 75002. Used with permission. Page 59: Reprinted with permission from the December 1942 Reader's Digest. Copyright © 1942 by The Reader's Digest Assn., Inc. Page 61: "Christmas Portraits" from *Christmas Remembered, Book Three.* Leisure Arts, Inc., toll free 1-800-288-8990. Price $24.95 plus shipping and handling. Used with permission. Page 69: Reprinted from *Home for the Holidays: Stories and Art for the Benefit of Habitat for Humanity,* edited by Gene Stelted and published by Peachtree Publishers, Ltd. Reprinted by permission of the publisher. Page 73: Excerpt from *A Gift of Sharing,* ed. Deborah Raffin, use by permission of Dove Books. © 1996 by Dove Audio, Inc.

CONTENTS

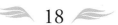
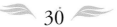

SEASON OF WONDER

I am the Christmas spirit!
I cause the aged to renew their youth,
and to laugh in the old, glad way.
I keep romance alive in the heart of
childhood, and brighten sleep with
dreams of woven magic.
I cause eager feet to climb dark stairways
with filled baskets,
leaving behind hearts amazed at the
goodness of the world.

E. C. BAIRD

SEASON OF WONDER

HARK!
THE HERALD ANGELS SING

Hark! The herald angels sing,
"Glory to the new-born King,
Peace on earth and mercy mild
God and sinners reconciled."
Joyful all ye nations rise,
Join the triumph of the skies.
With th' angelic host proclaim.
"Christ is born in Bethlehem."

CHARLES WESLEY

SEASON OF WONDER

My thoughts are drawn back,
by a fascination which I do not
care to resist,
to my own childhood.
I begin to consider,
what do we all remember best upon the
branches of the Christmas Tree of our
own young Christmas days,
by which we climbed to real life.

CHARLES DICKENS

SEASON OF WONDER

When Christ was born in Bethlehem,
'Twas night, but seemed the noon of day;
The stars, whose light
Was pure and bright,
Shone with unwavering ray;
But one, one glorious star
Guided the Eastern Magi from afar.

Then peace was spread throughout
the land;
The lion fed beside the tender lamb;

SEASON OF WONDER

And with the kid,
To pasture led,
The spotted leopard fed;
In peace, the calf and bear.
The wolf and lamb reposed together there.

As shepherds watched their
flocks by night,
An angel, brighter than the sun's
own light,
Appeared in air,
And gently said,
Fear not,—be not afraid,
For lo! beneath your eyes,
Earth has become a smiling paradise.

HENRY WADSWORTH LONGFELLOW

SEASON OF WONDER

Just as no snowflake
can be like another
so may it be said:
No Christmas can replicate another,
for each is special
and precious.

SEASON OF WONDER

Christmas is so many moods and
memories. . .
Christmas is the glitter of trees hung with
shining ornaments. . .
Christmas is the glow in the eyes of a
believing child.

LLEWELLYN MILLER

SEASON OF WONDER

The brilliant colors of Christmas that
begin to blaze at dusk. Whole
neighborhoods, so ordinary, taken for
granted, suddenly assume a gay and
profligate identity of light.
Rooftops are rimmed with rubies,
doorways are diamond-decked.
No sultan's palace could surpass their
splendor that spills even on to the shrubs
and hedges and trees in the yard;
such gaudy necklaces, such garlands of
brilliance—all clamoring "Look at me!"
Were these ever simply familiar houses
and yards? Will they ever be again?
No matter—for now, right now,
you live in Fairyland!

MARJORIE HOLMES

SEASON OF WONDER

THE JOY OF CHRISTMAS

SEASON OF WONDER

SEASON OF WARMTH

May the fire of this log
warm the cold;
may the hungry be fed;
may the weary find rest,
and may all enjoy Heaven's peace.

TRADITIONAL PRAYER SAID WHEN YULE LOG IS LIT

SEASON OF WARMTH.

Sing hey! Sing hey!
For Christmas Day;
Twine mistletoe and holly,
for friendship glows
In winter snows,
And so let's all be jolly.

SEASON OF WARMTH

Side by side or miles apart,
Christmas binds us
heart to heart.

SEASON OF WARMTH

Come Christmastime
the treasured gifts
are never made of gold,
Come Christmastime
the best bequests
are actually quite old;
a card arriving from afar
with news of something sweet,
a phone call with a greeting
from neighbors down the street.
As you can see
the best of Christmas,
the tried and the true,
are precious thoughts and wishes
like the ones I give to you.

SEASON OF WARMTH

"I will honor Christmas in my heart and
try to keep it all year....
I will live in the past, the present,
and the future."

EBENEZER SCROOGE'S PLEDGE
CHARLES DICKENS, *A CHRISTMAS CAROL*

SEASON OF WARMTH

Save a branch of your
Christmas tree
and use it to start the
New Year's fire.

ANNE WALL FRANK

How often have you caught a fleeting
waft of a scent and thought,
"That reminds me of Christmas!"
It might have been your uncle's cigar,
incense in a church,
a particular kind of soap that
a friend always gives you,
the smell of tangerines in the fruit bowl
or even the sage that you put
into the stuffing.
Then there is the piny scent of the tree,
the burning of those special apple logs
that you always reserve for Christmas day
or the warming smell of
the punch that greets you when
you arrive at a party.

GAIL DUFF

SEASON OF WARMTH

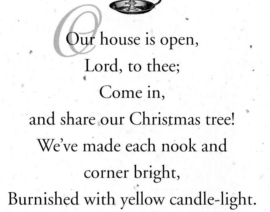

Our house is open,
Lord, to thee;
Come in,
and share our Christmas tree!
We've made each nook and
corner bright,
Burnished with yellow candle-light.

But light that never burns away
Is only thine, Lord Jesus, Stay,
Shine on us now,
our Christmas Cheer—
Fill with thy flame our whole
New Year!

LUCI SHAW

SEASON OF WARMTH

It is Christmas in the mansion,
Yule-log fires and silken frocks:
It is Christmas in the cottage,
Mother's filling little socks.
It is Christmas on the highway,
In the thronging, busy mart;
But the dearest, truest Christmas
Is the Christmas in the heart.

AUTHOR UNKNOWN

SEASON OF WARMTH.

Carol Brothers carol, carol joyfully,
Carol for the coming of Christ's Nativity.

As James Fisk Cushing grew up,
he eagerly awaited the day a family of his
own would make his Christmas complete.
As fate would have it, James matured
without meeting the woman of his
dreams. Discouraged and lonely,
the once-lively book publisher grew dour.
Then something wonderful happened:
Widow Elizabeth Anne Abbot and her
little boy Stephen moved to Bristol Falls.

SEASON OF WARMTH

Elizabeth quickly became fascinated
with the attractive man
and the two became friends.
To show his joy at having met her,
James secretly printed a new edition of
a holiday songbook and presented
beautifully bound copies to members
of the Bristol Falls Carolers Society
on Christmas Eve.
No one was as thrilled by the books
as Society member Elizabeth.
As the singers set off to begin caroling,
Elizabeth fixed her eyes on James
with unabashed adoration.
He, in turn, knew at that moment that
this would be his last Christmas alone.

ADAPTED FROM *A BRISTOL FALLS CHRISTMAS CAROL,*
BY GAIL DODGE

SEASON OF WARMTH.

SEASON OF FAITH

When they saw the star,
they rejoiced with exceeding
great joy.
And when they were come
into the house,
they saw the young child
with Mary his mother,
and fell down,
and worshipped him.

MATTHEW 2:10

SEASON OF FAITH

The people of Mexico call
the poinsettia the
"flower of the Holy Night."
A charming Mexican legend
explains its origin:
On a Christmas Eve, long ago,
a poor little boy went to
church in great sadness,
because he had no gift to
bring the Holy Child.

SEASON OF FAITH

He dared not enter the church,
and, kneeling humbly on the
ground outside the house of God,
he prayed fervently and
assured our Lord, with tears,
how much he desired to offer Him
some lovely present—
"But I am very poor and dread to
approach You with empty hands."
When he finally rose from his knees,
he saw springing up at his feet a
green plant with gorgeous
blooms of dazzling red.

FRANCIS X. WEISER

SEASON OF FAITH

In the bleak midwinter
Frosty wind made moan,
Earth stood hard as iron,
Water like a stone;
Snow had fallen, snow on snow,
Snow on snow,
In the bleak midwinter
Long ago.

Our God, Heaven cannot hold Him
Nor earth sustain;
Heaven and earth shall flee away
When He comes to reign:
In the bleak midwinter
A stable-place sufficed
The Lord God Almighty
Jesus Christ.

CHRISTINA ROSSETTI,
"HEAVEN CANNOT HOLD HIM"

SEASON OF FAITH

THE JOY OF CHRISTMAS

SEASON OF FAITH

In a cave on a windswept Italian
mountainside,
Francis of Assisi assembled the first
Christmas crib in 1223.

SEASON OF FAITH

The Christ child, placed on an altar
of stone, and two live animals—
an ox and a donkey—
were its only occupants.
Today, a tiny monastery surrounds the
cave, which still remains relatively
undisturbed by the years.

The idea behind the crib was to make
the story of Christ's birth more vivid
in the minds of shepherds and farmers
who lived there. The people were
enthusiastic. They were the ones who
suggested the ox and donkey.

MARK LINK

SEASON OF FAITH

For unto us a Child is born,
unto us a Son is given....

ISAIAH 9:5

SEASON OF FAITH

Though nearly two thousand
years have passed
since that glorious night
in Bethlehem,
the golden light shining from
the brilliant star,
sent by God to announce
Jesus' birth,
remains forever in the hearts
of believers throughout the universe.
God's promise is fulfilled!

SEASON OF FAITH

THE FRIENDLY BEASTS

Jesus, our brother, strong and good,
Was humbly born in a stable rude;
And the friendly beasts around
Him stood,
Jesus, our brother, strong and good.

"I," said the sheep, with curly horn,
"I gave Him my wool for His
blanket warm,
He wore my coat on Christmas morn,
I," said the sheep, with curly horn.

"I," said the dove from rafters high.
"Cooed Him to sleep so He
would not cry,
We cooed Him to sleep, my mate and I;
I," said the dove from rafters high.

SEASON OF FAITH

"I," said the cow, all white and red.
"I gave Him my manger for His bed;
I gave Him my hay to pillow His head;
I," said the cow, all white and red.

"I," said the donkey, shaggy and brown.
"I carried His mother uphill and down;
I carried her safely to Bethlehem town,
I," said the donkey, shaggy and brown.

And every beast, by some good spell,
In the stable dark was glad to tell,
Of the gift he gave Emmanuel,
The gift he gave Emmanuel.

AUTHOR UNKNOWN

SEASON OF FAITH

O, LITTLE TOWN OF BETHLEHEM

O, Little Town of Bethlehem,
How still we see thee lie,
Above thy deep and dreamless sleep,
The silent stars go by;
Yet in thy dark streets shineth
The everlasting Light;
The hopes and fears of all the years
Are met in thee tonight.

PHILLIP BROOKS

SEASON OF FAITH

There are some of us. . . who think to
ourselves, "If I had only been there!
How quick I would have been
to help the Baby. I would have washed
His linen. How happy I would have been
to go with the shepherds to see the Lord
lying in the manger!" Yes, we would.
We say that because we know how great
Christ is, but if we had been there
at the time, we would have done no
better than the people of Bethlehem. . . .
Why don't we do it now?
We have Christ in our neighbor.

MARTIN LUTHER

SEASON OF FAITH

SEASON OF JOY

*...*behold, I bring you
good tidings of great joy,
which shall be to all people.
For unto you is born this day in
the city of David a Saviour,
which is Christ the Lord.

LUKE 2:10–11

THE JOY OF CHRISTMAS

SEASON OF JOY

*L*ook skyward,
toward the Christmas moon.
Old Saint Nick's expected soon!
Sleigh bells ringing 'round his sled,
It's almost time to go to bed.
Leave Santa's treat to spread good cheer,
and don't forget his eight reindeer.
Sweep the hearth to clear the soot,
clear a path for Santa's foot.
Light a candle, point the way,
Santa Claus arrives today.

SEASON OF JOY

Next morning it was I who waked
the whole family with my first
"Merry Christmas!"
I found surprises,
not in the stocking only,
but on the table,
on all the chairs, at the door,
on the very window-sill; indeed,
I could hardly walk without stumbling
on a bit of Christmas wrapped up
in tissue paper.
But when my teacher presented
me with a canary,
my cup of happiness overflowed.

HELEN KELLER, *THE STORY OF MY LIFE*

SEASON OF JOY

Heap on more wood!—
the wind is chill;
But let it whistle as it will
We'll keep our Christmas
merry still.

SIR WALTER SCOTT

SEASON OF JOY

So remember while December
Brings the only Christmas Day,
In the year let there be Christmas
In the things you do and say;
Wouldn't life be worth the living
Wouldn't dreams be coming true
If we kept the Christmas spirit
All the whole year through?

AUTHOR UNKNOWN

SEASON OF JOY

We shall find peace.
We shall hear the angels.
We shall see the sky sparkling
with diamonds.

ANTON CHEKHOV

SEASON OF JOY

The holly's up,
the house is all bright,
The tree is ready,
The candles alight;
Rejoice and be glad,
all children tonight!

CARL AUGUST PETER CORNELIUS,
"DER CHRISTBAUM"

SEASON OF JOY

O Father, may that holy star
Grow every year more bright,
And send its glorious beams afar
To fill the world with light.

WILLIAM CULLEN BRYANT

Sing your song on Christmas day,

Let the season light your way.

SEASON OF JOY

Round the table
Peace and joy prevail.
May all who share this season's delight
enjoy countless more.

CHINESE BLESSING

SEASON OF JOY

Somehow not only for Christmas
But all the long year through,
The joy that you give to others
Is the joy that comes back to you.
And the more you spend in blessing
The poor and lonely and sad,
The more of your heart's possessing
Returns to make you glad.

JOHN GREENLEAF WHITTIER,
"THE JOY OF GIVING"

SEASON OF JOY

SEASON OF GOODWILL

There's more, much more to Christmas,
Than candle-light and cheer;
It's the spirit of sweet friendship,
That brightens all the year;
It's thoughtfulness and kindness,
It's hope reborn again,
For peace, for understanding
And for goodwill to men!

ANONYMOUS

SEASON OF GOODWILL

At Christmas play and
make good cheer
For Christmas comes but
once a year.

THOMAS TUSSER

SEASON OF GOODWILL

. . . some gifts I do hope to receive,
and some to give.
Gifts immaterial, but priceless,
and keyed to the tone of our times.
The gift of perspective,
and a saving sense of humor.
Of capacity to appreciate the good in
men without being sentimental,
and courage to accept their faults
without cynicism or despair.
The gift of understanding—
not the cold kind that is brewed in test
tubes or embalmed in textbooks,
but the sympathetic understanding that
springs from the heart.

BRUCE BARTON, "THE GIFT OF UNDERSTANDING"

SEASON OF GOODWILL

It is said that the custom of
hanging Christmas stockings by
the chimney stems from
the time St. Nicholas helped
a poor father with no marriage
dowries for his three daughters.
As the legend goes,
the good saint,

SEASON OF GOODWILL

wishing to remain anonymous,
went to their home in the middle of
the night and tossed three bags of
gold down their chimney.
Miraculously, a bag landed in each
of the girls' stockings,
which had been hung from
the mantle to dry.
Since that time, children the world
over have hung stockings and
awaited a visit with hopefulness
and excitement.

ADAPTED FROM "MOONLIGHT CALLER,"
CHRISTMAS PORTRAITS

SEASON OF GOODWILL

Abraham Lincoln's son, Tad, had a warm
heart. On Christmas Eve, 1863,
he approached his father, carrying an
armful of books received from his
parents. The boy told his father he
wanted to send them to soldiers.
"Do you remember how lonesome the
men looked?" Tad asked, for he had
accompanied his father on camp visits.
Lincoln thought for a moment before he
answered proudly: "Yes, son, send a big
box. Ask Mother for plenty of warm
things, and tell Daniel to pack in all the
good eatables he can, and let him mark
the box 'From Tad Lincoln.'"

MRS. JAMES S. DELANO, "RECOLLECTIONS OF THE
HOME LIFE OF ABRAHAM LINCOLN"

SEASON OF GOODWILL

I heard the bells on Christmas day
Their old familiar carols play,
and wild and sweet
the words repeat
of peace on earth,
good will to men.

Then pealed the bells more
loud and deep:
God is not dead, nor doth he sleep;
the wrong shall fail,
the right prevail,
with peace on earth,
good will to men.

HENRY WADSWORTH LONGFELLOW

SEASON OF GOODWILL

Selfishness makes Christmas a burden:
love makes it a delight.

Anonymous

SEASON OF GOODWILL

There's a ribbon 'round this
spinning world
that binds us like a tether,
It's woven of our true beliefs
and ties us all together.
Gift-wrapped, we stand a nation true,
and bound by pride and love,
For as we dance amid the stars,
we're cradled from above.

This Christmas, let us say once more:
We pledge to love our brother,
and let us live each day as though
we care about each other.
When all days become Christmas,
and strife is nevermore,
we'll thrive, a true community,
forever free of war.

SEASON OF GOODWILL

SEASON OF SPLENDOR

Winter birds sing
from the fencepost
over the glistening meadow,
where the sun breathes day
on the sleeping snow
of Christmas morning.

MARY ELLEN HANCOCK

THE JOY OF CHRISTMAS

SEASON OF SPLENDOR

Hang the wreath high,
this circle of holiday hope;
Showered with delights of the season
and symbolizing joy
that's never ending!

SEASON OF SPLENDOR

As the youngest of six children
from a very close family,
I always enjoy going home for the
holidays to spend time with
my mother and siblings.
Hanging out in the warmth and
familiarity of my mother's kitchen
brings back fond memories.

We all sit around the table eating and
telling stories, basically all talking at once
and therefore making a lot of noise.
It sometimes gets so loud that I get a
headache before the end of the night.
However, it is one of those comforting
aches, much like the sore muscles I have
after a really good workout.

BONNIE BLAIR, *HOME FOR THE HOLIDAYS*

SEASON OF SPLENDOR

Ah, the smell of Christmas cookies,
nothing's quite as sweet,
unless you count the helping hands,
who decorate each treat.
Each holiday we roll the dough,
and spread the luscious glaze,
We scatter sugar sparkles,
like splashes of sun rays.
The kitchen, full of wondrous smells
of spice and cookie art,
stays with me long past holidays;
this perfume warms my heart.

SEASON OF SPLENDOR

Everywhere—everywhere,
Christmas tonight!
Christmas in lands of the Fir tree
and Pine,
Christmas in lands of the Palm tree
and Vine,
Christmas where snow peaks
stand solemn and white,
Christmas where cornfields stand
sunny and bright...
Christmas where peace,
like a dove in its flight
Broods o'er brave men in the thick
of the fight;
Everywhere, everywhere,
Christmas tonight!

PHILLIPS BROOKS, *THE MEANING OF CHRISTMAS*

SEASON OF SPLENDOR

Yes, Santa Claus *does* come
down the chimney,
and there are eight tiny reindeer.
They live in your hearts ... and in mine,
when I see them in your eyes.

SEASON OF SPLENDOR

And yes, there are Christmas trees
from enchanted forests.

There are handmade ornaments,
sprinkled with fairy dust blown by a kiss.

There are nutcrackers that march,
and candy canes and sugar plums
that dance.

There are lights so bright,
the sky adds new stars each night.

There *is* magic to Christmas,
because you two make the magic happen.

With you, every day is Christmas.

ACTRESS JACLYN SMITH
(WRITTEN TO HER CHILDREN GASTON AND SPENCER)
A GIFT OF SHARING

SEASON OF SPLENDOR

73

Some say that ever gainst that
season comes Wherein our Saviour's
birth is celebrated,
This bird of dawning singeth
all night long;
And then, they say no spirit
can walk abroad;
The nights are wholesome;
then no planets strike,
No fairy takes, nor witch has
power to charm,
So hallowed and so gracious
is the time.

WILLIAM SHAKESPEARE, *HAMLET*

SEASON OF SPLENDOR

They bubble and flash,
they blink and glow,
the Christmas lights we love to show,
They're blue and white and red
and green,
The prettiest colors the world has seen.
We string them 'round our wreath
and eaves
and light our windows,
roofs, and trees
Each bulb, so lively, bright, and gay,
The Christmas glow that
lights our way.

SEASON OF SPLENDOR